SUPER ENGINEER

BUILD YOUR OWN BOATS

Thanks to the creative team:

Senior Editor: Alice Peebles
Fact checking: Tom Jackson
Design: Perfect Bound Ltd

First published in Great Britain in 2018
by Hungry Tomato Ltd
PO Box 181
Edenbridge
Kent, TN8 9DP

A CIP catalogue record for this book is available
from the British Library.

ISBN 978-1-912108-59-6

Printed and bound in China

Discover more at
www.hungrytomato.com

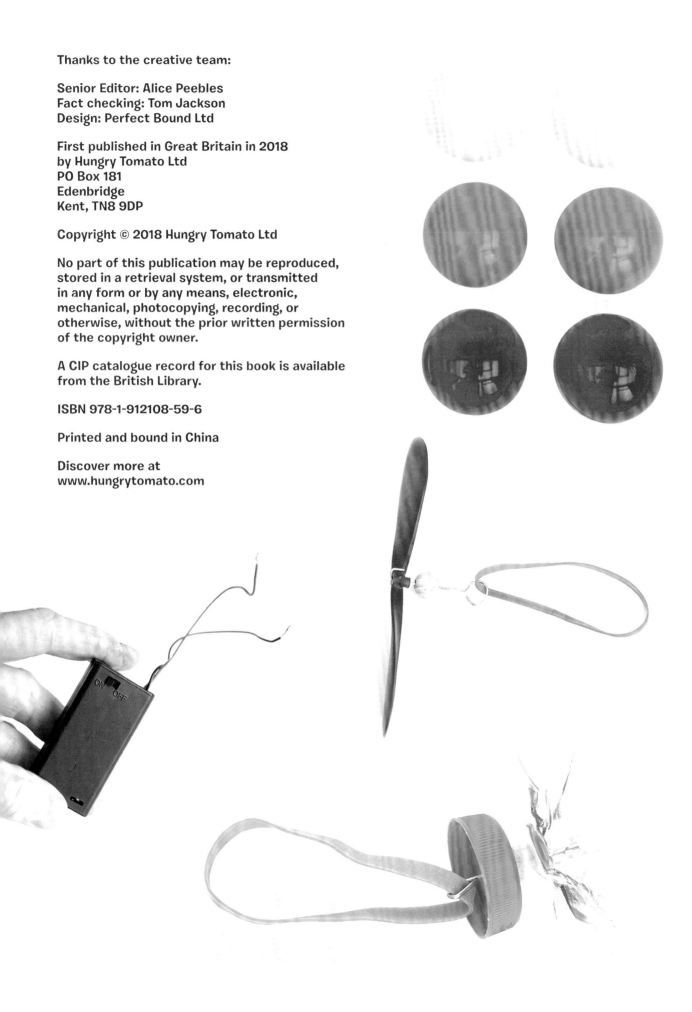

SUPER ENGINEER

BUILD YOUR OWN BOATS

BY ROB IVES

HUNGRY TOMATO™

SAFETY FIRST

Take care and use good sense when making these fun model boats – they are all quite straightforward, but you will need to cut materials, drill holes etc, for which it's handy to have an adult assistant (see below).

Every project includes a list of everything you will need to do it. Most will be stuff that you can find around the house, or is readily available and inexpensive to buy online or from a local hardware or general-purpose store.

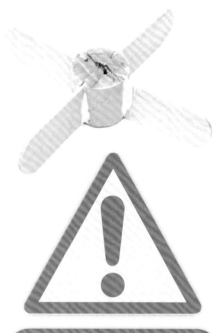

We have included 'How It Works' for each model, to explain in simple terms the engineering or scientific principles that make it move. And for some there is a 'Real-world Engineering' snippet that tells you more about actual watercraft (or water creatures!).

You may want to try them out at a local pond or paddling pool – so just make sure you take an adult to act as first mate. Even the captain hands over the wheel sometimes!

Watch out for this sign accompanying some model instructions. You may need help from an adult with completing these tasks.

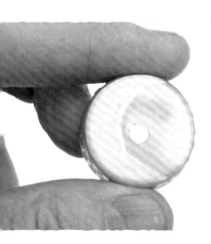

CONTENTS

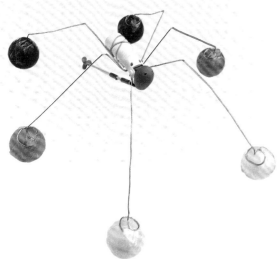

GLOSSARY ... 30
(Words in **bold** are explained here)

BOATS

It's often said that there's nothing half as nice as messing about in boats, or with boats – whether you go anywhere, or whether you don't.

Now you can build eight brilliant watercraft models and go on trips to the ocean deep – or maybe just the local pond or paddling pool (having trained up a trusty adult crew, of course). Or just try them out in your bath or inflatable garden pool!

Clamber aboard a twin-can catamaran or pootle in a paddle boat – driven just by elastic band energy. Add a motor to a leggy pond skater and a flat-bottomed swamp boat for extra zoom. Or just watch the breeze fill the sail on your raft and your sub slowly sink down, down down, then forge silently ahead, powered by a propeller, like the real thing.

So get your tools and materials together, start building and see how these boats move – and compare them to find out which is fastest and floatiest...

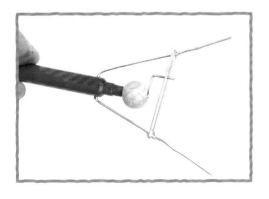

TOP TIPS

- Before you start on any of the models, read the step-by-steps all the way through to get an idea of what you're aiming for. The pictures show what the steps tell you to do.

- A project may need pencils to be cut into sections. Do ask for help with this and use a cutting mat, or similar surface to cut on. An efficient way to do it is to cut each face of the pencil in turn with a craft knife, then snap it apart. Tidy up any unevenness with the knife.

TOOL KIT

- Ruler
- Craft knife
- Gaffer tape
- Clear tape
- Tape measure
- Long-nose pliers
- Kitchen scissors
- Tracing paper
- Wire cutters
- PVA glue
- Epoxy glue
- Super glue
- Hot glue gun
- Craft drill

PVA

EPOXY

SUPER GLUE

COOL CATAMARAN

The 'cat' dates back to ancient Polynesia. Its lightness and stability have kept it very much in use – for fun, sport and naval operations.

YOU WILL NEED:

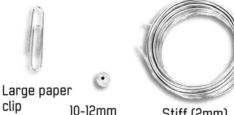

Large paper clip

10-12mm wooden bead

Stiff (2mm) garden wire

Two 130 x 50mm energy drinks cans

Large elastic band

Plastic propeller, 120mm long

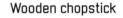

Wooden chopstick

Cable ties

TOOLS:
- Long-nose pliers
- Tape measure
- Wire cutters
- Gaffer tape
- Kitchen scissors

1 Use pliers to straighten the paper clip and make a loop at one end. Thread on the bead, then the propeller, and turn the wire end into a hook. Insert the elastic band in the loop.

2 Cut a 160mm length of garden wire, and use pliers to form a loop at one end and a hook at the other, as in the picture. This is the propeller wire and will attach to the other section as shown, but don't attach it yet.

3 Cut two pieces of stiff wire, 260mm long. ⚠️ Form them into two pairs of legs, bent as shown, with a 25mm loop. Bend the 'foot' ends inwards.

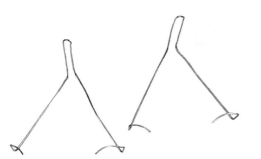

4 Tape the leg loops to the chopstick with gaffer tape. Tape the propeller wire to the other side of the chopstick. Tape the two cans to the 'feet' with the holes uppermost, and facing the same way as the propeller wire loop.

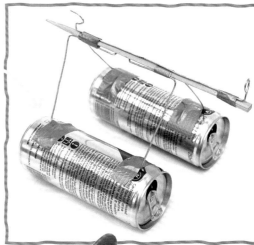

5 Fit the propeller section in place as shown. Fix on cable ties at each end for extra security, and trim the ends with scissors. Wind up the propeller clockwise from the front. Place the catamaran on water, release the propeller and...

...watch it go!

WHIZZZ!

HOW IT WORKS

The model uses an **air propeller** to drive it forwards. Air is forced backwards using the energy stored in the wound-up elastic band and this drives the model forwards. It's a simple example of Newton's Third Law of Motion: every push one way produces an equal push the opposite way.

REAL-WORLD ENGINEERING

Catamarans are very fast. The **hull** (bottom) is narrow to reduce contact with water, so there is less friction to slow them down. The double hull also makes them very stable. This means that the sail will not only stay up in strong winds, but can be larger than in single-hulled boats and so catch more wind.

SWISHY FISH

The fins have it! They're designed for speed, sudden turns, braking and keeping upright – probably the best bit of marine engineering ever.

TOOLS:
- Craft drill
- Long-nose pliers
- Ruler
- Craft knife
- Hot glue gun
- Wire cutters
- Kitchen scissors

YOU WILL NEED:

Cocktail stick

Four long paper clips

Water-soluble felt-tip pen

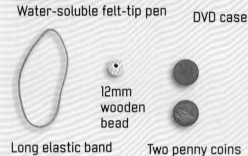
Long elastic band

12mm wooden bead

Two penny coins

DVD case

Polystyrene sheet offcut

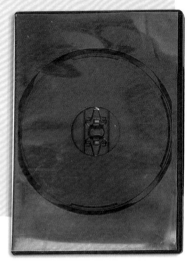

1 Pull the felt, the end and the tip out of the pen, leaving the plastic tube. Drill a small hole right through the tube 10mm from the tip with a craft drill. ⚠

2 Straighten out a paper clip with pliers. Bend the end over to trap the elastic band.

4 Thread the bead on the wire, then form a dog leg to keep it in place.

3 Cut 30mm off the cocktail stick. Thread the wire through the pen and out of the tip. Slip the stick through the end of the elastic band. ⚠

10

5 Straighten another paper clip, thread it through the two holes on the pen and bend it as shown. This will be part of the fish tail.

6 Make a thin wire loop, 40mm long, from another paper clip. Fix it to the tail wires using a hot glue gun, with the dogleg inside the slot. Trim the end of the dogleg with wire cutters. ⚠

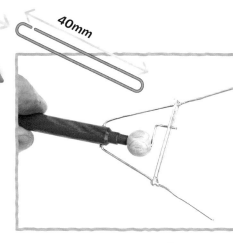

40mm

7 Use kitchen scissors ⚠ to cut and shape two identical lower body pieces from the DVD case, 85 x 25mm (at the widest). Glue the pennies to the inside of both pieces.

8 Measure the ends of the tail wires and ⚠ distance between them. Cut a curved piece of plastic from the DVD case to fit. Glue it in place.

9 Use a craft knife to cut ⚠ a 100 x 35mm piece of polystyrene for the upper body. Shape it as shown. Glue the body parts to the pen tube and allow to dry. Wind up the elastic band from the cocktail stick end.

Pop the fish in water and watch it swim!

SWISSH!

HOW IT WORKS

As the fish tail flaps from side to side, it sheds tiny **vortices** from the back and these move the fish forwards. Vortices are small whirlpools, fast-spinning areas of water within the water. Paddling a canoe also creates vortices.

REAL-WORLD ENGINEERING

Some fish are speedier than others. The tail fin gives propulsion (forward movement) and deepsea fish with a streamlined body and crescent-shaped tail fin are super-fast. Horizontal fins on their sides stop them rolling as they move along.

JETTIN' ALONG

The jetboat was invented by a New Zealand farmer for navigating shallow rivers. It's a high-speed craft propelled by a pressurized jet of water – but yours is moved by a special fizzy mix!

Small plastic fizzy drinks bottle

Vinegar

BICARBONATE OF SODA

Bicarbonate of soda

TOOLS:
- Kitchen scissors
- Epoxy glue
- Clear tape

Straw with flexible end

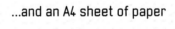

...and an A4 sheet of paper

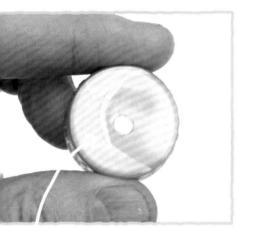

1 Use the point of the scissors to drill a hole in the lid of the bottle to take the straw.

2 Fit the straw in position just below the joint and fix it with Epoxy glue.

3 Pour vinegar into the bottle to a depth of about 20mm.

4 Make a cone from the paper, leaving an opening to fit inside the neck of the bottle. Secure with clear tape, and trim the top if you wish.

5 Add a heaped teaspoon of bicarbonate of soda to the vinegar.

6 Quickly screw on the lid – the solution in the bottle will soon bubble and fizz.

Transfer your boat to the water and watch it go with... **jet power!**

FFSSSHHH!

HOW IT WORKS

Pressurized foam from the vinegar-bicarbonate of soda mixture is forced out through the straw of the jetboat. This creates a **thrust** backwards that moves the boat forwards over the water.

REAL-WORLD ENGINEERING

Jetboats have a unit inside the stern (rear) that sucks up water, then pumps it out forcefully through a nozzle to push the boat along. They are speedy and have a shallow **draught** (portion of the hull that sits below the water), so are versatile and often used for fun rides.

PADDLE POWER

Boats powered by paddle wheels, rather than oars or sails, were used from Europe to China in ancient times. The first ones were driven by animals or humans – but all YOU need is an elastic band!

YOU WILL NEED:

Craft cork (not plastic)

Mint tin

Two wooden spatulas

Two pencils

80 x 3mm elastic band

Two cable ties

TOOLS:
- Craft knife
- Ruler
- PVA glue
- Kitchen scissors

1 Cut the cork in half with a craft knife. Cut four evenly spaced slots in the side of one half. Make them about 7mm deep. Cut four 40mm lengths from the spatulas, keeping the curved ends. Glue them into the slots in the cork with PVA glue.

2 Cut the points off two pencils with a craft knife. To do this, make a nick all the way round, then snap off the end.

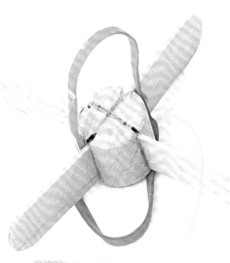

3 Tie the pencils to the sides of the tin with cable ties as shown. Trim off the ends with kitchen scissors.

4 Position the elastic band symmetrically on the cork as shown, so each side lies close to a spatula. Leave even loops of elastic on either side. Glue in place.

SPLISH!

5 Slot the pencils through the elastic band loops. Wind up the elastic band by turning the propeller a few times, away from the tin.

Place in the water and release!

HOW IT WORKS

When the boat is released, the elastic band unwinds, unleashing stored up energy. This makes the paddle revolve and dig into the water, pulling the boat forwards.

REAL-WORLD ENGINEERING

In a traditional paddle boat, a big **paddle wheel** at the rear or side rotated like a tyre and pushed water straight back, so the boat went forwards. The wheel was rotated by a steam engine, and could move forwards or backwards.

POND SKATER

It's fun to watch pond skaters whizzing about on water as if by magic. Now you can make your own cool motorized version that only moves when you want it to!

TOOLS:
- Craft knife
- Tape measure
- Wire cutters
- Long-nose pliers
- Gaffer tape
- Hot glue gun or Epoxy glue
- Clear tape

YOU WILL NEED:

Pocket battery-powered fan

35mm milk bottle lid

1mm garden wire

Six hollow plastic playballs, 55mm diameter

2mm heatshrink tubing, 35mm long

Straw

Elastic band

Wooden skewer

1 Cut out the disc of the milk bottle lid with a craft knife. Draw on a three-lobed shape for the propeller and cut it out. Make a small hole in the centre that will fit the wooden skewer tightly.

2 Use pliers to make up a 300mm length of wire into the shape shown. The sides of the U should match the length of the fan, about 55mm. Tape the straight end to the straw with gaffer tape.

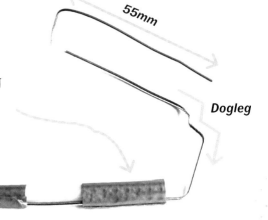

55mm

Dogleg

3 Pull the fan head off the fan to reveal the motor shaft. Join the skewer to the shaft with the heatshrink tubing.

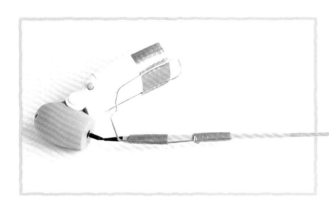

4 Cut off the bendy bit of straw and thread the skewer all the way through the straight section. Tape the looped end of the wire to the fan with gaffer tape. Glue the propeller to the end of the skewer with a hot glue gun or Epoxy.

5 Use wire cutters to cut three 700mm lengths of wire and bend them into a narrow U shape. Tape them together with gaffer tape just below the U bend.

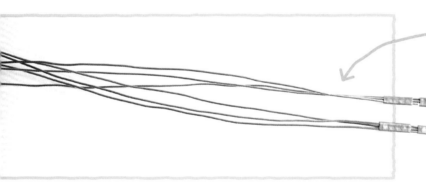

6 Separate the wires out evenly as shown, with the pair nearest the U bent back the most, the next pair in the centre, and the top pair facing forwards.

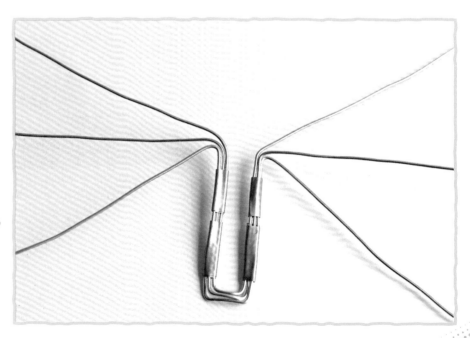

7 Bend the legs again so that they each have a 'joint' to look like six insect legs.

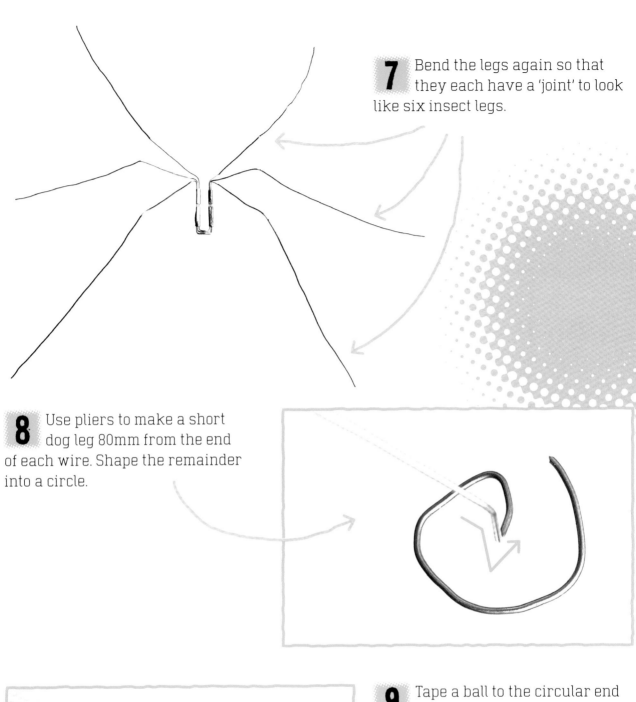

8 Use pliers to make a short dog leg 80mm from the end of each wire. Shape the remainder into a circle.

9 Tape a ball to the circular end of each leg using clear tape.

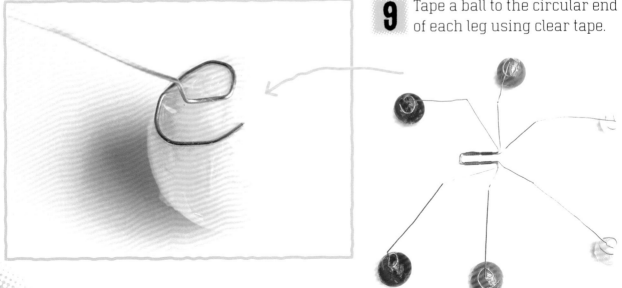

10 Fix the motor to the legs by wrapping an elastic band around both. (Using an elastic band rather than tape makes it easy to change the battery when necessary.) You may need to bend the wires to make sure the propeller sits just below the water surface.

Press the ON switch and watch your pond skater go!

BZZZ!

HOW IT WORKS

For an object to float, the force pushing it upwards from the water must be greater than the force pulling it down. This is called **buoyancy** or **buoyant force** and was described by **Archimedes**. The metal frame of the model would normally sink, but is kept afloat by the plastic balls, which have a high buoyancy. The propeller does the work of moving the model along.

Gravity

Object

Fluid

Buoyancy

REAL-WORLD ENGINEERING

Real pond skaters are insects that live on the surface of ponds. They don't actually use buoyancy to stay afloat, but rely on an effect called **surface tension**: a very thin, elastic layer on the surface of water.

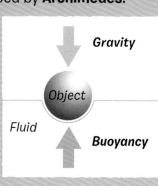

SAIL AWAY

A raft is the simplest of all boats, and in early designs, logs were lashed together with rope. Copy that idea using light materials to ensure total floatability!

TOOLS:
- Craft drill
- Ruler
- Craft knife
- Kitchen scissors
- Clear tape

YOU WILL NEED:

Thin (0.4mm) craft wire, 500mm long

Re-usable plastic shopping bag

15mm pipe insulation, 1,500mm long

Four skewers

Wooden chopstick

1 Drill a hole in the end of the chopstick with a craft drill to fit a skewer. Cut five 300mm lengths of pipe insulation with a craft knife.

2 Push the drilled end of the chopstick into the centre of one tube so it sits inside. Thread a skewer along the tube and through the hole in the chopstick. This will hold the chopstick upright.

3 Line up the remaining four foam tubes and thread a skewer through the sides, about 40mm from either end, to join them together.

4 Cut out a sail, 200mm square, from the plastic bag. Make a notch in the middle of the top edge, 30mm deep.

5 Fold this edge over a skewer and tape it down. Tie the centre of the skewer to the top of the chopstick with craft wire.

You're ready to sail the ocean blue!

6 Attach the bottom corners of the sail to the ends of the back skewer with craft wire. Trim off excess wire and the skewer ends with scissors.

HOW IT WORKS

The raft uses a buoyant material and its regular shape disperses weight evenly to keep it stable. The sail allows it to scud along before the wind!

REAL-WORLD ENGINEERING

Wind is moving air and is caused by differences in **air pressure**. Air under high pressure will move to areas of low pressure. The bigger the difference, the faster it flows and the stronger the wind. A square sail will 'catch the wind' but can only carry a craft in the wind's direction. A triangular sail can move across the wind to take you where you want to go!

DEEP DIVER

Imagine how strange it must feel to dive to the depths in a sub! Get a similar sinking feeling with a carefully constructed bottle sub, complete with propeller and hydroplanes. You're the COB (Chief of the Boat) and are in control of its 'bubble' (up or down angle).

TOOLS:
- Craft drill
- Tape measure
- Craft knife
- Long-nose pliers
- Wire cutters
- Scissors

YOU WILL NEED:

Large paper clip

600ml plastic water bottle

2-litre plastic milk bottle

300ml plastic fizzy drinks bottle

10-12mm wooden bead

Large elastic band

Thin (1.2mm) garden wire

1 Drill two holes in the bottom of the fizzy drinks bottle, one in the centre and one 10mm off-centre. ⚠️

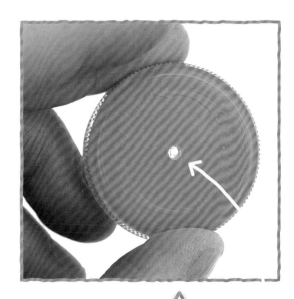

2 Drill a hole in the centre of the water bottle lid. ⚠️

3 Use a craft knife to cut out a five-blade propeller shape from the base of the fizzy drinks bottle.

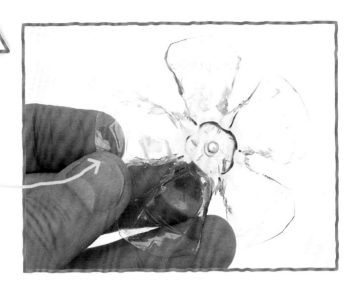

4 Use pliers to straighten out the paper clip. Make a hook at one end and loop the elastic band over. Thread the other end through the hole in the lid, the bead and the propeller. Secure the wire by twisting it and fit the lid on the bottle.

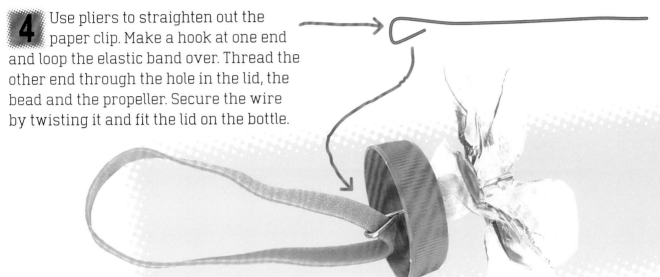

5 Make a hook in the end of a 400mm length of wire and push it through the centre hole in the bottom of the bottle. Hook it over the elastic band and pull it into the bottle to about 25mm from the bottom.

6 Use the pliers to bend the wire into a loop as shown and cut off any excess with wire cutters. Push the free end of the wire into the off-centre hole to secure it.

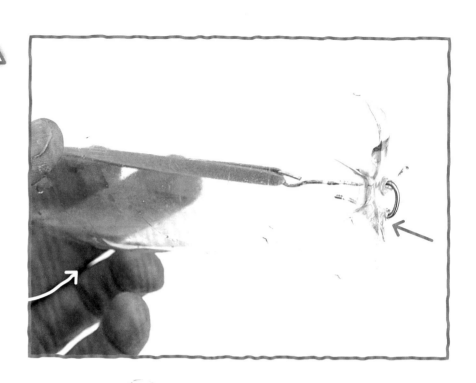

7 Push a skewer through the walls of the bottle, above or below the elastic band, leaving an even length on either side.

HOW IT WORKS

Since the bottle is light and has high buoyancy, it needs water to weigh it down and take it below the surface. You can decide how much to add according to how far it sinks and how far you want it to sink! The propeller does exactly the same as a real sub's propellers, only it rotates by elastic-band power, rather than an electric motor.

CROSS-SECTION OF A SUBMARINE

Outer hull filled with water: sub sinks

Outer hull partly filled with water: sub hovers

Outer hull mainly filled with air: sub rises

8 Cut two **hydroplanes**, 60 x 90mm, from the milk bottle. Make two small holes near the short edges with scissors and thread the vanes onto the skewer.

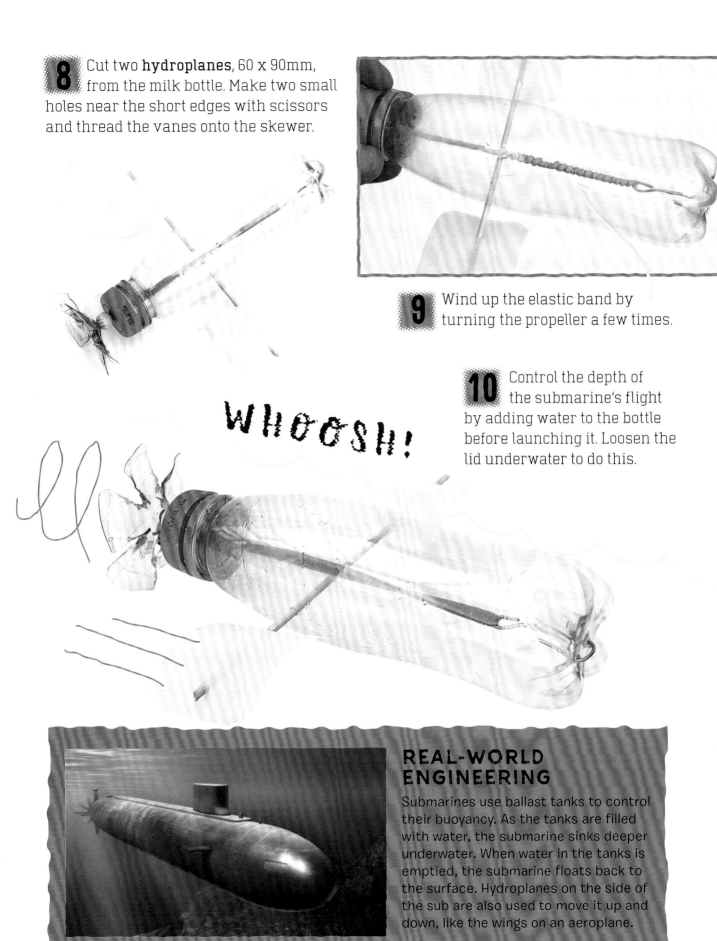

9 Wind up the elastic band by turning the propeller a few times.

10 Control the depth of the submarine's flight by adding water to the bottle before launching it. Loosen the lid underwater to do this.

WHOOSH!

REAL-WORLD ENGINEERING

Submarines use ballast tanks to control their buoyancy. As the tanks are filled with water, the submarine sinks deeper underwater. When water in the tanks is emptied, the submarine floats back to the surface. Hydroplanes on the side of the sub are also used to move it up and down, like the wings on an aeroplane.

SWAMP BOAT

Want to explore the Florida Everglades or the mangrove forests of Malaysia? What you need is a swamp boat! With this cunning craft, you'll never get tangled up in all that low-growing greenery.

YOU WILL NEED:

Craft foam

Polystyrene offcuts

Two skewers

Two cable ties

TOOLS:
- Craft knife
- Tracing paper and pencil
- Super glue
- Craft drill
- Ruler
- Scissors
- Hot glue gun

Corrugated cardboard offcuts

Large paper clip

3V electric motor

Craft cork (not plastic)

3v battery holder with switch

...and two ballpoint pens

1 Cut a cork in half lengthwise with a craft knife. Cut a slot on each side of one half, so that they're angled in opposite directions.

2 Use this template (actual size) to trace and cut two propeller blades from craft foam. Fit them into the slots and secure them with a dot of super glue.

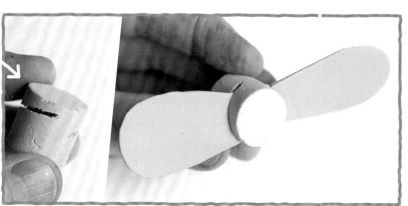

BLADE template

60mm

27mm

3 Drill a small hole in the centre of the cork to fit tightly over the motor.

4 Fit two batteries into the battery holder.

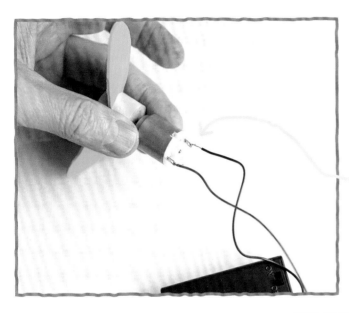

5 Wire up the motor to the batteries, red to the positive and black to the negative terminal.

6 Use a cable tie to join them together to make a power unit. Trim the end of the tie with scissors.

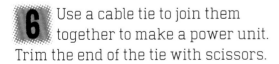

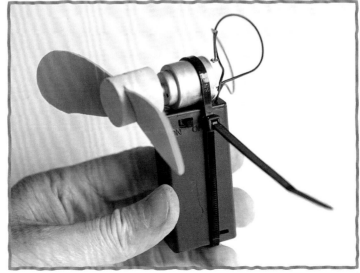

7 Use the templates (not actual size) to trace out a hull and prow. Cut two hulls and one prow from polystyrene with a craft knife. Glue the hulls together with a hot glue gun, then glue on the prow.

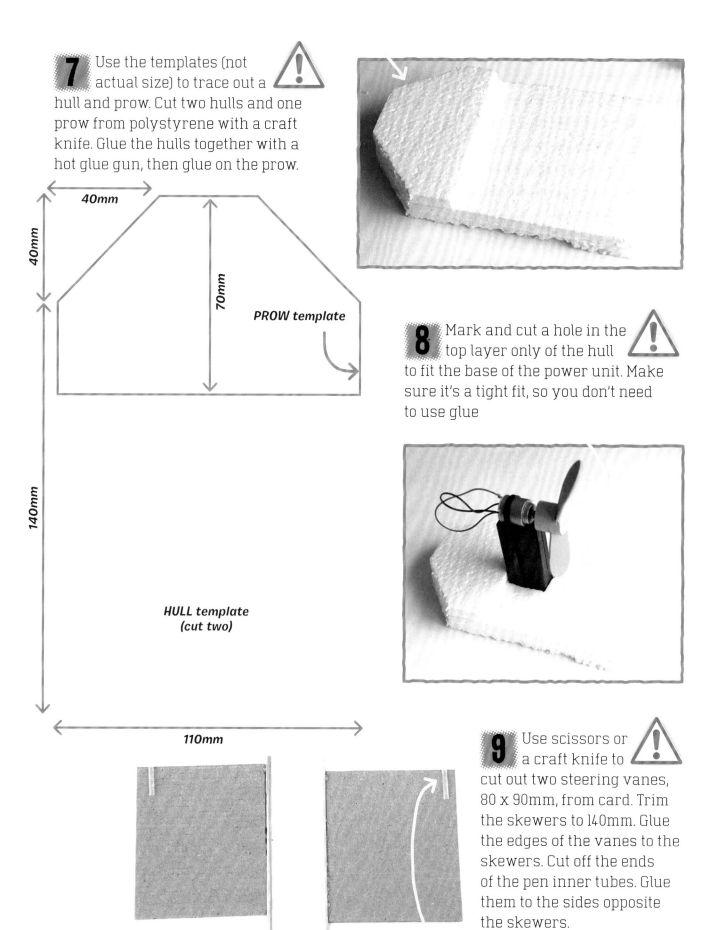

40mm

40mm

70mm

PROW template

140mm

*HULL template
(cut two)*

110mm

8 Mark and cut a hole in the top layer only of the hull to fit the base of the power unit. Make sure it's a tight fit, so you don't need to use glue

9 Use scissors or a craft knife to cut out two steering vanes, 80 x 90mm, from card. Trim the skewers to 140mm. Glue the edges of the vanes to the skewers. Cut off the ends of the pen inner tubes. Glue them to the sides opposite the skewers.

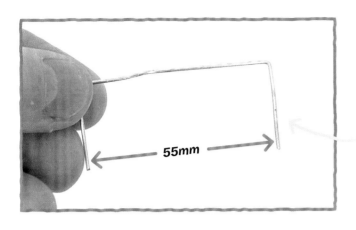

10 Use pliers to straighten out the paper clip and shape it as shown.

←— 55mm —→

11 Fit the vanes to the back of the boat, 15mm from the sides. Join them together by slotting the ends of the paper clip into the pen inner tubes.

Launch your boat in a swamp, switch on the motor and dodge the crocs!

VSSSHHH!

HOW IT WORKS

You can try out your boat on a weedy pond and see why its flat bottom is so practical – it won't get stuck in the weeds. For the same reason, the propeller is on deck rather than submerged as in other boats – so the swamp boat's operating parts can work freely. The boat is steered by pushing the vanes in the direction you want.

REAL-WORLD ENGINEERING

Real swamp boats are made from very buoyant materials so that they float high in the water. They have a shallow draught and are moved by a big propeller that creates a column of air pushing backwards. The operator makes the air column move left or right with a stick, and sits high up to get a good view of obstacles ahead.

GLOSSARY

AIR PRESSURE

The weight of air at any given point. It depends on its density, or how close together the molecules are. Warm air is less dense and creates less pressure so it rises; cold air is denser and creates more pressure.

AIR PROPELLER

A shaft mounted with two or more blades and powered by an engine to rotate, which provides the force needed for lift and movement. The pitch or angle of the blades may be varied according to the required speed and air resistance. The word comes from the Latin *pellere*, meaning to push or drive.

ARCHIMEDES

Mathematician and engineer of ancient Greece, famous for working out the law of buoyancy (see below), also called Archimedes' principle. It's said that he figured this out while lying in his bath! He is the founder of hydrostatics, the study of fluids, and is credited with inventing the Archimedes screw. This is a machine for moving water from a lower to a higher level.

BUOYANCY, BUOYANT FORCE

The upward force exerted on an object fully or partly submerged in a liquid (or gas), also known as Archimedes' principle. The buoyant force is equal in magnitude to the weight of the fluid displaced by the object. For example, a ship sinks into the sea until the amount of water it displaces (pushes aside) equals its own weight. A heavier ship will displace more water, and be kept afloat by the equivalent buoyant force.

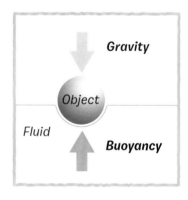

DRAUGHT

The distance between the surface of water and the lowest point on a vessel's hull. This varies widely in watercraft, depending on what they are built to do. A shallow draught vessel is needed for shallow water, and where there are submerged plants or objects. A deep draught vessel is able to carry heavy loads and remain stable in the water.

HULL

The lower part of a ship that floats in the water. There are different shapes of hull – flat, rounded or V-shaped – and the lowest part is the keel, which runs like a backbone along the centre.

HYDROPLANE OR DIVING PLANE

A flap on the side of a submarine that helps it to submerge. It acts like a wing but works in water, not air. There is usually a pair fitted on either side of the bow and stern (front and back), which allows the sub to be angled up or down.

PADDLE WHEEL

A large steel-frame wheel, fitted on the outside with evenly spaced paddle blades. It is rotated by an engine to provide thrust, and the lowest quarter is always underwater. The Romans used a type of paddle boat, and it was the main means of transport on calm tracts of water such as lakes, and the big rivers of the USA throughout the 19th century.

PROW

The pointed front of a boat or ship, also known as the bow.

SURFACE TENSION

The elastic effect at the surface of water created by the way the water molecules are attracted to each other.

THRUST

The powerful force produced by a machine in one direction that gives it an equally strong movement in the opposite direction. In a space rocket, for example, burning fuel creates a mass of gases under pressure. The gases have to go somewhere, so they blast out the back with a force strong enough to propel the craft up and away from Earth.

INDEX

THE AUTHOR

Rob Ives is a former maths and science teacher, now a designer and paper engineer living in Cumbria, UK. He creates science- and project-based children's books, including *Paper Models that Rock!* and *Paper Automata*. He specializes in character-based paper animations and all kinds of fun and fascinating science projects, and often visits schools to talk about design technology and demonstrate his models. Rob's other series for Hungry Tomato include *Tabletop Battles* and *Amazing Science Experiments*.